MAKE THE MEDIA WANT YOU

AN INSIDER'S GUIDE TO CREATING PERSUASIVE PITCHES

VETERAN BROADCASTER

LISA BRANDT

Make the Media Want You: An Insider's Guide to Creating Persuasive Pitches

LBCS

VoiceofLisaBrandt.com

ISBN (eBook) 978-0-9881582-5-2
ISBN (5 x 8 paperback): 978-0-9881582-4-5

Edited by Jennifer D. Foster, Planet Word

Foreword by Mark A. Rayner

MAKE THE MEDIA WANT YOU

AN INSIDER'S GUIDE TO CREATING PERSUASIVE PITCHES

Foreword

by Mark A. Rayner

Let me tell you a secret that I haven't told anyone else. It's a secret that could raise a few eyebrows: I love audio more than any other medium.

That might seem like a weird thing for a writer of fiction to admit, but it's true. There is something just so intimate and immediate about sound. It's my preferred method of putting information into my brain. Sure, I still read books, and watch television, and, hell, I'm even enjoying this internet thing everyone's connected to constantly. But decibel-for-decibel, audio is my jam.

And, if you're trying to publicize something, it should be yours, too, whether you're doing your own publicity or PR for a client.

We live in an attention economy. That means there is so much content out there, getting the attention of anyone is a challenge. So, how do you get your signal through all that noise?

One answer is good audio. It can cut through distractions and forge a direct relationship with your audience. Whether you're an author trying to encourage people to buy your book, a politician advocating a new policy direction, or a business owner selling smart widgets, the intimacy of audio will help you connect with listeners. These listeners are your potential customers, business partners, and free word-of-mouth advertisers.

Because of that intimacy, I think it's one of the best ways to tell a story.

My career has been about telling stories. I've published four novels and two collections of short stories. In addition to working as an author of books, I am the Program Coordinator of the Master of Media in Journalism and Communication at Western University. We help budding journalists and communicators learn to become kickass storytellers in all media. I teach the social media and digital production course in this program. Plus, I teach web design, information architecture, and other nerdy things in the Media, Information and Techno culture undergrad program, as well as the Library and Information Science master's program.

I'm *supposed* to love *all* forms of media, but I'm here to tell you, audio is the one that you cannot ignore if you want to click with your audience. Hearing your voice will give them a sense of who you are and why the information you're telling them matters. So, yes, that might raise some eyebrows.

Lisa Brandt has been a media fixture in my hometown of London, Ontario, for years. I'm always impressed by the quality of her interviews, how she can pull the best out of her guests.

And I finally got to meet her while I was hawking my third novel, *The Fridgularity* at a local Chapters bookstore. The store was having a local authors event, and Lisa was there selling copies of her memoir, *The Naked Truth*, which is an insightful and funny story about her time working at a nudist resort. Since meeting her, I've appeared on her morning show at CJBK, and we are mutual fans.

Lisa understands the ins-and-outs of how to use audio to tell a story. She has spent a career working in broadcasting, and her advice in this book is based on years of observation.

"Your idea needs a story," she says in the preface. It's not enough to have a great idea, an interesting book, or a new gizmo that you want to share with the world. You need to have a story that will connect your audience to it emotionally.

Lisa's prose is filled with examples that will help inspire you to make your story compelling. She uses real-world examples of how to go about getting the attention of a host or producer. (In some cases, these are stories that demonstrate what *not* to do.) Her advice is concrete and to the point, just like your pitches to the media should be.

She has also included practical advice from other hosts and producers, either as quotes or as whole chapters with their own examples. These help to flesh out and reinforce her views on how best to engage with the media.

Chapter One deals with how to get on the air in the first place: how to make your pitch enticing, and how to make the life of the broadcaster easier. Remember, they don't owe you anything. In fact, given my experience on both sides of the microphone, I'd say it's the guest that has the greatest responsibilities in this phase.

Chapters Two and Seven have advice from other broadcasters.

Chapters Three through Five cover:
- tips for charities and non-profits
- how to do off-site events
- how to make the most of social media

That leads to Chapter Six: how to manage the interview. Her advice here is a great primer for how to be an excellent guest, so you can make the most of the opportunity.

This book cuts through the clutter and gives you advice on how to publicize your event or product in a way that will help you thrive in this distracted world.

Preface

To the untrained eye, it's not obvious that the hit American reality TV series *Shark Tank* offers terrific examples about how the media respond to requests to appear on their shows and in their pages. There are striking similarities. A Shark might think a business concept is brilliant, but it's not in their wheelhouse. They typically invest in clothing, for example, and this business centers on food. There's nothing that this one Shark can offer to help the food business grow, so they declare themselves "out." In another case, a Shark might not believe there's a market for whatever the business is selling. They don't buy into the concept. Once again, they'll be "out" and won't make an investment. The more the business owner tries to sell an idea to a disinterested Shark, the less patient the Shark becomes. They said no. They know themselves and what they believe, based on experience, will make them money. Most often, the person pitching their business will continue fine without the Shark, and sometimes they're fueled by the rejection. You can't win them all.

Every day, media professionals are deluged with e-mails, social media posts, phone calls and other messages containing pitches for — in my case, as a former radio show host— airtime. Sometimes, what's offered is of value. Other times, it is not, but perhaps it will be to someone else. The media must keep its listeners, viewers and readers in mind while making these decisions. Our audience is to us what money is to Sharks.

The editorial decisions about what makes it into the final cut are in the hands of the hosts and producers of the show. Those working for big media chains are sometimes accused of being puppets on strings, as if those decisions are handed down from an ivory tower. In my own experience, in markets big and small, that's just not true. Sometimes, a corporate group gets behind a cause. For example, Corus Feeds Kids, an annual initiative that raised millions across the corporation's properties. The hosts were expected to devote airtime to it. But day-to-day editorial judgments aren't usually dictated from above. Media employees haven't been told to follow a certain point of view or political bias. There are exceptions, of course, and they are obvious. But distrust in "major media" as a collective, biased blob is naive at best and ignorant at worst.

However, we are expected to appeal to our target audience and deliver what they will find important or interesting.

As the one pitching to the media, you must make a business case for yourself or your client. Routinely, broadcasters, hosts, and journalists are doing the jobs of two or three people, and in some cases, more. Everyone's budgets have been cut to the bone. Print journalists are sometimes their own editors. Where editors no longer exist, paginators – those who lay out the pages including editorial content and ads – have at times taken their place. Where editors do exist in broadcasting, producers also have other responsibilities. They produce more than one show, and they're juggling different mandates and preferences for each one. Podcasters are often solo acts. They're researching, booking, selling, marketing and, oh yeah, hosting, editing, and uploading their shows. The workload has never been heavier, and competition has never been fiercer. Everyone is expected to do more with less, and that means they don't have time to peruse a detailed dossier on every pitch that comes in.

Despite these limitations, media pros still put out pretty darn good products with a fraction of the people power they used to have. That's because they genuinely care about delivering high quality content and maintaining their reputations. There's a saying in radio: "You're only as good as your last show." That's not entirely true because we have all done shows so bad, they ought to have been our last! But the desire for greatness is there while the relentless demands continue to consume everyone's time.

Before you contact a member of the media about your event/idea/product (outside of purchasing advertising), keep these three realities in mind:

1. **No one owes you airtime or an article**. They understand that your cause or invention or issue might be a worthy one. But please refer to who the most important customers are —listeners, viewers, and readers. If someone doesn't leap at the opportunity to put you on the air or in the paper or magazine, do as the great Kenny Rogers once sang, fold 'em and walk away. You might have success with someone else.

2. **Outside of a pre-interview for major network television, many don't have time to meet with you to discuss a pitch.** Sometimes dozens of pitches arrive in a single day. If media

professionals met with everyone, well, they'd never sleep. As a morning show host, I didn't sleep anyway. If you can't explain in a few e-mail sentences why there will be interest in what you're offering, there will be no interest. You've heard of the "elevator pitch"? You should be able to condense the salient points of your pitch and its benefits to a decision maker in the time it takes to ride an elevator between a few floors. If it takes longer than that, you haven't edited it well — it's not succinct. Everyone's time is valuable. Don't hold someone hostage while you dither.

3. **Your idea needs a story.** If you want attention, your story must be compelling but honest. A story is much more interesting than a statistic. People love to hear about other people. For example: "There are more than 120 distinct types of brain tumors." That piques my intellect, but my emotions remain untouched. Then there's Stephanie's story. Doctors diagnosed Stephanie with a brain tumor called pilocytic astrocytoma at three years old. She has undergone two major surgeries, with lasting repercussions. Stephanie's balance, depth perception, fine motor skills and sensory discrimination have all been affected

by her brain tumor. But despite being told her future would be limited, Stephanie hasn't let her medical history stop her from fulfilling her dreams. She is currently working toward her third degree, a Master's in hydrology at the University of Saskatchewan, after which she looks forward to time off, travel and work in the field of natural sciences. Could I please talk to Stephanie? She sounds amazing. When Stephanie tells her story, people will listen. Her perseverance will touch their emotions and keep them interested. And that sought-after donation to brain tumor research is more likely to follow.

Your pitch doesn't have to be about someone in a fight for their life. It doesn't need to concern the biggest or the best of anything. The wacky, crazy, silly stunt is passé, although there will always be a place for it, too. Hit us in the feels. Teach us something worth knowing. Introduce us to someone extraordinary. Bring us a solution to a widespread problem. Explain why you're a perfect fit for a podcast's genre. There are hundreds of ways to make your story matter. Find one of them. If you can do that, you've got a shot at grabbing attention.

In the following pages, I'm going to tell you what I've learned in more than three decades of booking guests for radio shows and selecting people for television and print interviews. Now, I cohost a podcast and these guidelines holds true for podcasts as well. Some of my experienced friends in the media will also offer their perspectives. This is a no-frills how-to manual about how to deliver a worthwhile pitch and how to be a great guest. These tips are not absolutes; they're best practices. Perhaps *you* can deliver a fully cooked turkey to a host and get some airtime (that anecdote will come later!). But this guide is meant to give you a sense of what it means to be in the media, as well as some ideas on how to better prepare the pitch before you offer yourself or your client for a guest appearance.

This was a conversation I had that inspired me to finally write this book after thinking about doing it for years.

> CALLER TO MY OFFICE: Hi Lisa! I want to come on your radio show.

> ME: Okay. What do you want to talk about?

> CALLER: Well, I have a clothing business, and I want to talk about that.

ME: Oh, that's advertising. You need to talk to our sales department about purchasing airtime.

CALLER: No, no, no. I just want to come on and talk. I am doing stuff for charity.

ME: Okay. What stuff?

CALLER: Well, for everyone who buys a certain amount from me, I'll donate to charity.

ME: So, you want to come on and drum up new customers?

CALLER: Exactly!

ME: Sorry, but that's what our clients do through radio ads. That's something you must pay for.

CALLER: No, no, no. Maybe you can think of some way I can work my business into your programming?

This is not the way to approach a busy host or producer. Someone's vague, manipulative attempt to worm their way into the show with nothing for our listeners except a sales pitch simply won't cut it. We don't have the time or the inclination to create a marketing plan for your business. That's your job. (Or you can consult one of our sales professionals who will be glad to do it, when you are buying airtime.)

We meet a lot of people in the media. Because we had a conversation at a golf tournament once, doesn't mean I owe you a service that everyone else must pay for. This type of attempt never ends well. Networking is important, but it won't make an unworthy idea worthy of airtime. And we resent feeling used.

Plus, we don't want to undermine our sales department. The reality is the media are in a fight for survival. I couldn't and wouldn't put a paying client's competitor on the air "just to talk." In fact, when I was on the radio, if I needed expert commentary on a type of business, I would go to our clients before asking someone who didn't invest in us. It's just a smart business move, and I don't apologize for it. The first people we support are the ones who support us. Remember, private broadcasting is funded solely by advertising revenue.

This doesn't mean that people who don't advertise won't get on the air — far from it. But there must be a legitimate reason that doesn't undercut sales, and you need to know the difference. I always wanted to put interesting people on the air. To tell fresh stories and make radio content that mattered to people. But I wouldn't sacrifice my mission to provide entertaining, informative programming that was listener centric just because someone called and pressured me to. If there was nothing in a talk segment for my listeners but a client's wish to make more sales, it wasn't going to get a green light.

Many of us preferred to source our own guests and shuddered at the mere thought of being one of one hundred radio shows that would have Mr. X on in the same week. However, there are exceptions to every rule, and a well-crafted pitch that speaks to something that interests people is a gift we'd be foolish not to accept.

I was blunt and direct with people who were ill-prepared when they attempted to make a pitch to come on the air. With the demands on my time, I couldn't afford not to be firm. I tried to be kind, but I'd tell it like it was, and that's what I aim to do with this book. None of these approaches is a guarantee. They do offer, however, a better path toward your goal — getting coverage. I hope you find it valuable.

Chapter One

From Idea to Airtime

TIMING

Everyone books their show a little differently. Some programs, such as those in my last radio format of news/talk, don't mind a last-minute idea, especially if it concerns something topical. Breaking news is exciting, and those in that genre know how to pivot when necessary. They are constantly looking for fresh angles on current stories, and one that's interesting enough can always get worked into the program.

But everyone appreciates lead time. In other words, don't wait until Friday to tell everyone about your

Saturday event. You've been living and breathing all the details you're about to spring on those who are just learning about it. Media people work on strange schedules. Living in the moment is one of the things that radio does best but it's better to have some breathing room. Frankly, if you're not approaching the media until the last minute, you need to develop better organizational skills and/or priorities. (And read the rest of this book!)

> *"I once got an e-mailed press release at 11:30 a.m. They wanted me to come to their event at 1 p.m. Another time I got an email for an event that was 20 minutes from when the email was sent. What I take from that is they don't want to be taken seriously. The days of reporters sitting around waiting for the phone to ring (or an email to arrive), if they ever existed, are long over. PR/ communications folks should assume the reporter they are pitching already has at least a couple of assignments on the go for that particular day." Dan Brown, veteran journalist.*

Outside of breaking news, most interviews don't happen organically. They require some research or fact-gathering. Most of us know a little about a lot of things but we're not necessarily PhDs.

Consider how many minutes there are in an hour and how many hours in a show. We must plan and fill all that time, and your segment would be just one of — in most cases —several in a day, five days per week. Even if you have provided a compelling argument and piqued someone's interest enough to get on the air, you are going to be on for one segment. The hosts and guests need to distil and refine what they will be sharing down to the most salient points. If you want to use ten thousand words and dream that you'll captivate the world with your story, write a blog post. Radio and TV, in most cases, aren't the places for long-form, super-detailed information. (More about being on air is coming later.)

The radio is still going even after you turn it off. Believing that a show happens off-the-cuff is a tremendous compliment, but also naive. Hosts and producers plan, arrange, and prepare as much as they can, so that they can sound informed. It's not foolproof, but only a fool would go on the air without preparation for their program.

My former show, for example, is based in news. (It's still carrying on fine without me!) We didn't *have* to have guests on unless they were part of the current news cycle, could offer more depth to a story or brought us a fresh perspective. In other words, we could get along fine without you or your client/subject. This is true for most shows when it comes to guests the hosts and producers haven't sourced on their our own. And it's why you need to make the guests and subjects matter to us and convince us — quickly and succinctly — the benefit your guest/idea/subject will bring.

Podcasters who rely on guests to interview are looking for what we're all looking for: authentic, compelling storytellers who fit the show's mandate. Don't approach the host of a podcast about camping if you want to talk about make-up. Make sure it's a fit.

THE PITCH

What should be in your pitch? The five Ws: who, what, where when and why. And your why should be why it matters to our end users, our listeners/viewers/readers. Make us care about it. And do it simply.

Many media relations teams do a terrific job of explaining complex research and topics in everyday terms. Their communications pros know that hosts and journalists aren't scientists, CEOs, or financial whizzes, so when they send us a news release on a study, they break it down into layperson language. If they merely sent research results, journalists and producers would likely — always — pass on the story. They have neither the time nor the desire, frankly, to go through complicated material only to discover it might not be worth covering due to a lack of audience interest.

Every day, journalists and hosts receive the equivalent of science-speak when someone is so immersed in their own world that they can't or don't know how to explain why it would matter to anyone else. In my case, when producing and hosting a radio morning show, I didn't have the luxury of time. I couldn't devote precious minutes or hours probing complicated documentation when my on-air partner and I were filling twelve segments a day as producers, researchers, guest-getters, oh yeah, and hosts. We wanted to talk about the hard stuff and delve into deeper, important material. But if we couldn't find the relevance in a few sentences, we knew it wouldn't make compelling radio.

Another thing some PR pros do well is to get out ahead of predictable events. They know that we are planning, and they dovetail their experts seamlessly with our topics. An election is coming up: Here's who we have available for interviews in the poli-sci department. A celestial event is about to happen: Here's contact info for an astrophysicist who can explain it.

> *"Don't send out a media release at the end of the day, just before you're about to leave the office, or head into a meeting. You're reaching out to us; make sure you're available. Same goes for listing a media contact. If that person isn't around to speak to the issue, pick a different contact or wait*

until they're available." —Robyn Brady,
CKXS Wallaceburg News Director; former
Community Relations Coordinator, Ontario
SPCA's Chatham-Kent Animal Centre.

Avoid industry jargon in your communication. Police department communications officers are famous for writing in police-speak, and some of that insider-only verbiage has made it onto the airwaves. "Execute a search warrant" is my personal favorite. Are police in the habit of going in to search a residence without a warrant? And who says "execute" in this context? Only the police. Lazy or inexperienced writers copy that wording verbatim. But I digress.

Unless a term has made it into the mainstream, don't deliberately use terminology that requires those outside of your industry to ask for a definition. It's a bit like vague booking[1] on Facebook: annoying! Be clear. Don't assume that we know as much as you do about your organization. Tell us what you have and what you want. Use friendly language. Give the appearance of someone we'd like to share a small studio with for a while.

I've had guests assume I'm a moron and others who thought I must have several degrees in every discipline. The truth is most of us are somewhere in between. We

---

1 Vague-booking: posting an item without revealing details. For example: "I can't wait for Wednesday!" Readers are meant to wonder what's happening on Wednesday and ask for more info.

are curious, eager professionals who know a little about a wide range of topics. And we love learning.

Keep it brief. Imagine we're having a conversation, and your goal is to keep me from getting bored and looking at my phone. What's the best aspect of your client or idea? You don't want to lose my attention, so keep the dull, irrelevant details to yourself.

Don't make me do math. Give me percentages or fractions. Tell me why they matter and to whom they matter. I will know whether those people, whoever they are and however they're defined, are part of my target audience.

If your story concerns the elderly, then you're talking about the parents of my listeners. The approach should come from the point of view of those adult children, not as if the elderly are my listeners. Some publicists, speakers and others supply sample questions. That's fine, but don't be surprised if they're not all used. Many of my colleagues and I prefer to do our own research and formulate our own questions. We don't want our interviews to sound like everyone else's, even if no one who hears them knows — we will. Providing bullet points about highlights is much better.

Please don't ask for the questions ahead of time. There are a couple of reasons why this is a frustrating demand. First, it shows that the guest doesn't know their material well enough to be spontaneous. That's concerning. Second, while we may, indeed, work from a prepared list, we also listen to your answers, and sometimes that inspires a question we hadn't thought of before. Forcing us to stick to a list would take away everything we love about doing great interviews — spontaneity, creativity and living in the moment. Making a human connection. Also, imagine how much it would add to our workload to prepare question lists for every guest. We run lean and mean, and when you ask for questions, you are demanding that we do even more work. I promise you that no one is going to ask you to do or say something impossible or deliberately make you look like a fool. (Unless you're the subject of a scandal, or a politician, and then all bets are off.)

It's nice when someone has bothered to find out my name and title and got it right. Personally, I don't judge mass e-mails too harshly if they're managed well. However, a mass e-mail does make me wonder whether my competition will also book your guest.

A publicist once sent me an interview confirmation e-mail on which my direct competitor was also copied. The e-mail included specific details about our separate bookings of the guest. My competitor noticed that I had booked an earlier timeslot than his, and he cancelled his interview. This was a strategic mistake on the publicist's part. Had they not sent that e-mail, we might never have known. Whether they were trying to save time, I'll never know. It was a foolish error.

And please, use the BCC field if you are sending out a mass e-mail. (Police, fire, government of all levels, this includes you!) Save us from scrolling through the address of every media person we've ever heard of and keep our e-mail addresses to yourself. The BCC field exists to help cut down on spam and other worthless messages. Use it, please.

If we respond to your e-mail, please read ours. A reply isn't necessarily a guaranteed booking. Sometimes we are looking for more information.

Here are two examples that show the consequences of the difference between reading the e-mail and not reading the e-mail.

1. Children's performers Splash'N Boots were coming to town to perform several shows. We didn't usually book interviews with kids' acts, but after asking around for parents' familiarity with the duo and finding it high, we decided to invite them on. However, instead of a regular interview, we suggested that they participate in our weekly segment titled "Ask Me Anything." It was a departure from a traditional Q&A, included listener involvement, and it offered a peek behind the curtain of a fascinating

job or hobby. The publicist saw the value, and Splash joined us for the segment. She was delightful as the subject of "Ask a Children's Performer Anything." She had us howling with laughter as she told stories of single fathers, toddlers in tow, attempting to pick her up after shows. Splash's publicist had read our idea and was savvy enough to agree to it as an entertaining way to promote their shows.

2. A music artist coming to our city was offered to us on the morning of his live show. I wrote back to ask for clarification about the show. It was described as a private event, and its purpose was unclear. I was attempting to ascertain whether our listeners could still buy tickets. (Remember: what's in it for _them_ is my first concern.) Instead of answering my e-mail, the contact forwarded it to the artist, his manager, and his agent. That was followed by an onslaught of e-mails from all three. They assumed the on-air visit was a done deal — although that was never even implied, much less stated

— and began tossing me dates and times when the artist could phone in. I had to be firm and explain that we wanted a live in-studio appearance or none. I felt manipulated by the original contact and forced into a situation that required me to be the bad guy and "cancel" an interview that had never been booked. Don't ever do that. I won't forget, and I will find it hard to forgive.

HOUNDING AND BRIBING

If we don't feel that your idea or client will work for us, it might work for another show whose target audience is more in sync with what you're pitching. That show might even be in another timeslot on our radio station. Hosts and producers share ideas and suggest guests to each other all the time. (We did that on my last station, at least.)

> *"Stop e-mailing or calling fourteen times a week about the same idea — 'just following up!' I'm busy, and if I didn't say yes to your pitch the first time, I'm not likely to on the umpteenth time." — Jason White, radio reporter/anchor*

The perception that we'll wear down over time is faulty. Driving us crazy isn't going to work. We talk to each other, and you don't want to be known as a pain in the butt. Word will get around. Suck it up and move on. You are in sales - selling yourself - and salespeople must accept rejection.

Context is important. A soon-to-be best-selling cookbook crossed the desk of a colleague who remarked, "Ugh, a cookbook on the radio!" I took a closer look and noticed that it was *Yum & Yummer* by Greta Podleski, half of the sister duo behind the huge sellers of the *Looneyspoons* and *Crazy Plates* cookbooks. That idea went from zero to hero in a flash because of the author's history. The publicist had done a fantastic job of explaining the book and the sisters' previous successes. The interview was great. Who doesn't love to talk about food? Sometimes, a little genuine and legitimate context can help. If there is a history or a provenance to what/who is being offered, explain it up-front.

While we're on the subject, let's talk about details. Earlier I suggested that we shouldn't be bored by details. However, leaving key details out isn't wise, either. I've only been ambushed on the air twice, and there's nothing those people can do to restore their reputations with me. Please don't lie by omission.

Here's a fabricated hypothetical example. A group is attempting to convince the provincial government to end funding of the Catholic school system. The group claims it's what most people want. However, another group comes forward and claims its poll shows that most want funding to continue. But to make their findings more interesting, they leave out the fact that they only polled parents whose children are going to Catholic schools. If I had conducted that interview only to find out later that those who were polled were completely biased, I would have been terribly upset and felt betrayed.

When it comes to choosing subjects, it really isn't about only what the hosts and producers like or don't like. (The exception is talk show hosts with a political point of view.) I tried to get into the shows *Game of Thrones*, and *This Is Us*, but neither one of those mega-hits hooked me. Still, I am aware of their popularity and impact on pop culture. Even though I don't watch them, I know enough about them to get by, and accept that I'm in the minority. It would have been foolish of me to ignore these huge television phenomena on our show.

You could fit what I know about running marathons on the head of a pin and still have room left over. However, my last radio partner was a dedicated runner who competed in triathlons and other competitions. Therefore, I developed an interest in the topic, and we knew from the response that a portion of our audience was interested, too.

Media pros are ready to learn, eager to be convinced. They're trying to be great, unique, and informative. Help them get there.

Here's another way to look at what works better on radio. Every time I hear a car ad that says something to the effect of, "We've got to clear out last year's models." or "We need to sell two hundred cars this month." I think wasted opportunity. A car buyer doesn't care what the car dealer wants to do. They want to know what a car dealer will do for *them*.

If I were going to write a commercial for a car dealer it would go something like this:

"You know that feeling you get in the pit of your stomach when you walk onto a car lot? The one that tells you that you're going to get taken advantage of. You don't know how, and you don't know when, but at some point in this transaction, it's going to happen. Not at XYZ cars. I'm Fred Flintstone, General Manager, and my friendly sales staff will treat you with respect, transparency, and courtesy — or you can ask for me by name, and I'll make it right. At XYZ, we don't care about selling you any car. We care about getting you into the car that's right for you and doing it without broken promises and hidden costs that pop up at the last minute. XYZ cars. We're not like the other car dealers. See for yourself."

That's a commercial that would speak to me and my trepidations about buying a car. It's not about the dealer and what they want. It's about dealing with this customer's deepest concerns and solving that problem. That's what radio does. It's intimate and one-on-one.

If you learn one thing about radio here, let it be this. Anyone who says, "Hello, everyone!" on the radio has already lost their chance to connect with the listener. I emphasize listener, not listeners, because — as I said — we talk to one person at a time. It's likely how you listen: in the car, in the kitchen, in the bathroom, on a jog, at your desk. Often, it's just you and the radio.

What is going to get you on the air if you're not famous? Relevance. A great story. An aspect of a current news story that's unusual or personal. A rare event or a challenge. A milestone or major anniversary of something in pop culture that you're an expert on. The explanation of something we all wonder about or know so little about that we will be surprised to know. An overlooked local person we should get to know. The possibilities are endless, and it's all in the presentation.

By relevance I mean relatable to the audience. Does it appeal to the target audience? You're a small business owner who's upset about an upcoming jump to your tax rate, and that's been dominating the news cycle. You've started a petition. You've considered the many ways your business will be affected. Your opinion might be worth hearing. You're going to attempt to golf one hundred holes in one day and break a local record that's stood for forty years. You're the founder of the first-ever tech firm in the city and are celebrating your thirtieth anniversary; you're credited with attracting other like-minded businesses and creating hundreds of jobs. You want to talk about what it's like to be a pioneer in your field and inspire others to take a chance on becoming an entrepreneur.

If you're pitching a blood donor clinic, find me a person who has just made their one thousandth donation. A craft show? Tell me about a crafter who climbed vines in Indonesia to pluck the specific flowers she uses in her work. There is nothing as boring as reciting the date, time, and location of an event, and yet that's all most people are prepared to do. Offer something more compelling.

It's no wonder that former radio hosts and stand-up comedians make great podcasters. They know how to tell a story and keep someone's attention.

Bottom line: you have a fully formed idea. There is something in your pitch for our listeners, our number one concern. You don't have to follow a template or have an English degree to communicate well. Just be clear. Don't be vague. Don't say you'll explain yourself if I would just give you a call. I won't call you. While you're teasing me, know that I have a dozen clear and present details in front of me that need my attention. We don't have time for games, and many of us live on weird hours. We can't always call you when you want us to.

Also, bribes aren't effective.

As I drafted this book, I worked for a media giant that expressly forbade us from taking freebies in exchange for airtime. I fully supported this rule and abided by it without exception. In the old, old days, you could get a mention on the air by sending something free to an announcer. No one seemed to mind if a free pizza arrived, and we gave a shout-out to its maker. Times have changed. Ad dollars are more difficult to release from clenched hands. We do not give away our product — airtime — as easily, and hosts aren't allowed to take goodies in exchange for doing so.

Trinkets and treats haven't always worked, anyway. When I was a midday talk-show host in a medium-market city, an inexperienced PR person pitched me an idea for a guest I turned down. It was near Thanksgiving. When that day's show was over, reception called to tell me I had a visitor. I hate the pop-in visit to begin with and find it disrespectful. As I emerged from my office, the smell of Thanksgiving dinner filled the hallway. There, at the reception desk, was the PR guy holding a huge tray that contained a foil-covered, freshly cooked turkey. It was mine! All I had to do was book his client. Who wouldn't take the gift of a turkey? Me. I thanked him for the effort but had to send him away with his bird. Not only was I forbidden to accept it, but it also didn't make his idea for my show any more appealing. I was also insulted that he felt he could sway my intellectual decision.

PAPER ISN'T WHAT IT USED TO BE

There are those who still believe that "the paper" is the media authority in any given city. Facts no longer support this. It remains true only in certain big cities and to an older generation. Newspapers do excellent jobs of long-form investigations (where they still have the budget for it), and op-ed columns, but their subscription numbers have plummeted. Competition comes from all over, including broadcast media such as radio, television, and social media. We're at least a couple of generations deep into media consumers who don't get the same joy out of holding a paper in their hands.

Referring on air to reading something "in the paper" sounds as antiquated as it is rude to a broadcast news organization. This is the reality of our business, and guests have been invited into that reality. It's important to know for a successful visit and the possibility of a return visit. If you refer to your news source as "the paper" while you're on a news/talk-radio station, you won't be thought of fondly. No one is asking you to be dishonest. They're asking you to be respectful.

It's also weak sauce to cite an appearance in the local newspaper as the reason we should pay attention to your client or idea. Remember, we want to be on top of things, but also different from the rest. We also don't want to be a follower or late to the party. This might not be the case in smaller markets, where there are fewer local stories to tell. The paper picked it up first and radio can follow. However, radio has an old, outdated reputation for "ripping off" newspaper copy. I am adamantly opposed to taking a print journalist's writing and using it verbatim on the air. (Remember, the genre was news/talk. Admittedly, not all hosts share my view.) It's archaic and as wrong as if it happened the other way around. Journalists put sweat equity into their work, and radio should respect that.

I wrote a newspaper column that papers carried nationally for many years. One day, a friend alerted me to the fact that a major market talk show host was discussing my latest column on the air. He was ripping it to shreds and disputing its content. That part didn't bother me. The problem was he didn't once name the publication or the writer – me. So, you can be sure that I know how it feels to have my work "stolen" for someone's entertainment.

A listener once chastised me for not "sticking up for" a competing radio station. The other station was being sued by a politician who alleged one of its hosts had libeled him. After the same politician appeared on our show, we received an angry listener e-mail. "I thought you guys stuck together." was his comment. No sir, the opposite is true. Most of us at competing stations know and even like each other, but when it comes to competition, we don't mess around. I will defend my station and its brother stations, but never, ever help those with whom we compete. It's a fight for survival, as dramatic as it sounds. Two of the early radio station stops on my tour of duty no longer exist because they were no longer viable. Radio station frequencies are getting powered down — forever. It's survival of the fittest.

Chapter Two

Erin Davis—From the Host's Perspective

Get the names right. Get the station right. Get the titles of the hosts right. And the gender. And the spelling. We're performers — with the accompanying ego necessary to put ourselves in the ring every day — and we half expect you to pretend to know us. So don't tick off your targets before you've even pitched. For example: a long-time market staple and beloved midday host, a man named Sandy Hoyt, got more than one letter from a PR company addressed to Stan Hoyk. It happened twenty-plus years ago, and I've never forgotten. As for me, my co-host and I were known as "Don and Erin," and we enjoyed a number one spot in a very tough ratings market. Which would explain, I guess, the mailed pitch I got one day addressed to Donna Nerin. I kid you not. (But at least I recycled).

Yes, methods by which pitches and ideas are sent out have gone electronic, but getting names, titles, genders and even radio station call letters wrong is unforgivable in this age of instant information.

Thanks in advance for putting together what we all hope are cohesive, brief, and entertaining talking points. But for the love of Zeus, don't call them "DJ Chatter Points." Although that's what you might consider what we do, many of us don't consider our discussions — even the fun ones — to be "chatter." In many or most cases, a lot of thought and preparation go into what we present on the air. So, when you call it "chatter," it's dismissive. You may not mean it, but it can be.

Make sure we have all the details that we need and won't have to go searching the Internet for the location of your charity set-up or something as basic as that. Make this easy for us; increasingly media are in the position of having to do two- or ten-people's jobs, so please be clear, concise, and accurate. The more information you give us, the more likely we are to share it and <u>do so with accuracy</u>.

Put yourself in our shoes. Would you want to talk about bad breath for fifteen minutes or sock rot or whatever product it is that you're pitching to cure what ails our listeners? Oh, you would? Then find an angle or two to help us make it intriguing, helpful, entertaining and worth a listener's time! Don't make us create your pitch for you. We just don't have time!

Also, consider our audience. Don't try to get me to book a sex-related interview when our listeners are all soccer moms and dads with their children in the back seat of the car, listening to the radio together. I recall our senior producer being hounded year after year by a local PR guy who just wanted to get his clients, Playboy models, on the air, on our show. He finally lost it on the PR guy and asked him if he didn't know that ours — the biggest in the city —was a FAMILY station? It didn't end well. But the discussion needed to occur. Know who we are before you pitch, because we are there to respect and serve our target audience. — Erin Davis, renowned Toronto morning show host

Chapter Three

Charity and Not-for-Profit

You're raising money for a charity. That's wonderful. You've written a song about a tragedy. Good for you. It was cathartic. We hope it does well. But those things in and of themselves are not enough reasons to put you on the air.

It's not that we don't care; we do. Radio stations devote hundreds of hours a year to charitable causes. I used to emcee charitable events on my own time because I thought they were important, and I wanted to take part in them. I have also ghostwritten and provided voice-overs for material for several charities without payment or credit. We all help where we can. But we don't have to cover an event simply because it's for a charity. There are only so many hours and so much airtime. That's not to say your event isn't worthwhile. But if it's for a micro-cause that draws a handful of people, a mention on our online calendar is the best we can do this year. Again, we have our listeners' best interests at heart.

Fundraisers of some sort are held every week of every year. Unless you are personally touched by the cause, details about these events can be, frankly, terribly boring to listen to. A laundry list of sponsors followed by the date and time of an event, especially a walk or fun run, may fulfill a need for you, but it's dull and repetitive for us. We cannot feed our audience a steady diet of similar dishes.

However, a person who has battled back from the disease that you're raising money to fight might not be boring. It always comes back to storytelling. So, instead of pitching the idea of only promoting your fundraiser, offer a live and local person who offers a reason – a human connection - to get interested in the event. They had a long wait time for treatment or they're battling the government to cover their massive medication costs, or they've overcome tremendous odds and want to help others who are still fighting the same disease. A remarkable story from a well-spoken person to whom we can all relate is a surer path to compelling radio. The details of the event will still get airtime wrapped in an interview that will touch listeners' hearts. The same goes for print.

Again, people love stories about other people, not necessarily about free hot-dogs and face painting for the kids.

As for your song, if it's worth hearing, people will let us know. If I had a dime for every time a budding songwriter (or their parent) thought a tribute song was a surefire entry to radio airtime, I'd have retired long ago. It doesn't cost anything to put your song on YouTube and spread the word on social media. If it's good, it will get noticed and shared. If it's good enough, it will go viral and catch the media's attention. Or, you'll have something more upon which to build a pitch. In most cases, we are not in the business of breaking artists. We are in the business of informing and entertaining listeners and getting ratings. It's a jungle out there, and we can't allow everyone to swing on our vine.

Finally, please don't go over our heads to get on the air. Some publicists make their pitch to the boss and hope that he or she passes it along to staff, and that's fine. But to go there after we have turned you down, in a bid to get a different answer, is just crummy. It's also foolish. You're the outsider and we are all colleagues. Who do you think will be looked upon poorly in this scenario? Our managers trust us to make the right decisions. They have their own fish to fry, and their fry pan is already full of fish.

Chapter Four

Off-site Events and Interviews

You're holding a news conference to make an announcement. It's a demonstration of some great new tech gizmo or the opening of a business. Whatever it is, the same tenets of compelling media coverage apply. Lead time. Storytelling. And in this case, good organization of the details ahead of time.

> *"Please give some consideration to the media when sending out an invitation, whether it's for a ribbon-cutting ceremony or a major funding announcement. Anything less than twenty-four hours' notice is a bit insulting. We understand it takes a lot of time and*

organization for you to put a news event together; you have a dozen moving parts that must be coordinated to make an announcement, but so do we. It feels, at times, that inviting reporters to a media event is something of an afterthought." —
Robyn Brady

If it's a typical announcement, we'll be subjected to "a few words" from every company executive who wants their time at the mic before we get to the meat of the story. We know when you're holding us hostage, and we expect a little of that.

We want to know who the main spokesperson is so that we can get what we need: audio, video, quotes. Sometimes we're granted early interviews to hold under embargo until the announcement is made. These are wonderful opportunities given to reporters who can't make it to the actual event or prior to it, to allow them time to meet their deadline. Most honor the embargo request. If someone doesn't and releases the information early, unless it was an honest mistake, I wouldn't trust them again.

Have you ever noticed that when a politician wants to make a point about something, they often go to someone's home and talk to a family about the issue? They know that a politician talking at a podium can be the audio and video equivalent of paint drying. But real families with genuine problems, whose members are looking to that politician for a solution, make the politician seem sympathetic and helpful. It's a brilliant strategy, and that's why it's used so often with satisfactory results.

Whether it's someone's home, an office, or wherever your announcement is being staged, we have fundamental concerns. When we arrive, will we be able to plug in to a main audio board? Or will there be room at the front for us to get our gear close enough to whoever is speaking? And most importantly, will there be cookies? I'm kidding about the cookies. (Sort of. Cookies have never gone uneaten!)

There are so many kinds of on-site announcement-type events that it would be impossible to make suggestions for each category without starting another book. But remember this: television needs something to look at. A person at a podium can only be on-screen for so long before viewers start nodding off. Give TV motion and action. It's the same with print; photographers need eye-catching photos. And for radio, we need all of that in the form of sound. So, give us someone who knows the story inside and out, and who doesn't get tired of repeating it over and over as they submit to interviews with each journalist. A spokesperson who doesn't understand that we will all ask questions we already know the answers to, will make our job that much more difficult. Make sure they're seasoned enough to know how it all works. I'll never forget the company spokesperson who barked at me, "That's right in the press kit. Didn't you read the press kit?" He wasn't made aware that he'd have to repeat highlights from the press kit for us to have something to put on the air in audio form and I had to gently explain it to him. Don't put a client or a journalist in that position. It makes the client look incompetent and annoys the journalist.

Chapter Five

The Social Network

We can help each other via social media. But you can hurt yourself, too, if you don't understand us well.

Several times someone has included our Twitter handle and the handles for one or more of our competitors in the same tweet, then wondered why they had no reaction from any of us. Here's the reason. You won't get a like or a retweet from one of us if both of us are in the tweet. This goes back to not wanting to show any public love to our competition. If you name our competition, even alongside us, we'll pretend it never happened. That's how competitive media companies are.

Do a bit of research and find out who owns whom. Make notes if you must. (Media properties tend to change hands.) One Christmas, our radio station received several mailed cards addressed to all the hosts at a competing station. No one is perfect, and people make mistakes. But just understand that they get noticed.

Sometimes, posts on Facebook tag all the media in the area because they're meant to draw our attention to the information and nothing more. That's fine. In that case, we appreciate being included and drawn to the post. But if you're looking for social media love in the form of sharing and liking, you will be deafened by the sound of silence if you think we're going to share something that also features a tag or handle for our competitors.

If you promote your appearance with us before, during and after the fact, we'll give you some social media love in return. We love giving and getting clicks, likes, and retweets.

I try not to be too precious about photos of me, but it's always nice to be asked before they're posted. Sometimes a photo that looks fine to someone else highlights the one thing about me that I can't stand. Say, my cowlick or my short stature. An intern once posted an unflattering video of me while we were on location in a coffee shop doing a "pay-it- forward" campaign.

The video began with three excruciatingly long seconds of my back filling the entire screen. Unbeknownst to me, the designer blouse I was wearing shared a houndstooth pattern with a shirt worn regularly by Ricky in the *Trailer Park Boys*. A savvy viewer posted a photo of Ricky in the same shirt below the video on Facebook. I had to laugh — it was very funny. But it would have been better if the video had been edited to show the important stuff, not a sea of black-and-white patterned fabric. On an unrelated note, I have a designer blouse for sale.

Asking before posting goes both ways. Your friendly media professional should extend the same courtesy to you.

So, what is the best way to use social media to attract attention? And which platform should you be on? I've tip-toed onto TikTok, but I still don't see how it will benefit my business of doing professional voice-overs and providing written content to magazines and websites. So, let's consult an expert.

Kevin Bulmer is the President of NSM Brand Media in London, Ontario, Canada, Kevin lives and breathes marketing, branding, and social media. He and his team have elevated the reputations of a wide range of companies in all sorts of industries. From dental to real estate to – you name it.

There's no substitute for life experience, and Kevin has already accumulated enough for a couple of lives. He is known for several things including his songs, as a singer/songwriter/recording artist and live performer. He's a former radio host and broadcast media consultant. He cofounded an event management company and was the manager of a NASCAR-sanctioned racetrack, all while being a devoted Dad to two boys who are now young men. He's a sought-after public speaker and business coach.

I began by asking how a business owner, entrepreneur, artist, or anyone else choose which social media platform or platforms to use? Put another way, is it better to shoot with a shotgun and hit everything or use a rifle and just hit one or two?

Calling on our shared history in radio for an analogy, Kevin says it depends on what fits your brand, has your audience, and supports your content.

"It's not all that different from matching up clients with a radio station. They might like rock. But if they're selling something that's more rural, then they should look at the country station.

"It also depends on whether they are business to business, or business to consumer. Are they mostly or completely local? Or are they ecommerce so that they're regional? There are lots of questions to answer first.

"If you're business to business then LinkedIn is a no brainer. Everybody that we work for uses some combination of LinkedIn, Instagram, and Facebook. Google My Business is becoming more of a priority. We've only got a couple that that post videos to YouTube.

"TikTok for instance is hot right now, but not everybody is going to be doing video. Certainly not everyone's going to do video in the volume that TikTok seems to want. I haven't seen a whole lot of evidence yet for people just expecting their local store to be there."

Because Kevin didn't mention Twitter, I asked whether that platform was passe.

"We have one client that we post to Twitter for and that's only because they already had a Twitter channel. And they wanted it to look like it was being kept up to date. As opposed to, if somebody visited their Twitter channel and tumbleweeds were blowing through."

Kevin and his colleagues see Twitter as a different animal in the social media jungle. He likes to get in and get out of it quickly, and unscathed by the political fights and other nastiness that Twitter's become known for.

"I follow about five people who cover my favorite basketball team, The Miami Heat. I check what they're saying about the games. And I follow Kevin Harvick during the NASCAR races. And I'm very, very disciplined about not clicking on anything that's trending hashtag. It's just too easy to go down the rabbit hole."

Out of date social media pages dot the digital landscape. So, how do potential followers and customers view social media pages that are left untended?

"You need consistency and quality of attention. If you've got links on your website to your social pages, people go there and it's obviously out of date you're better to just take it down. Choose one or two and mind the store."

If you're on any social media, you find yourself checking on whether your latest post is getting likes or comments. I asked Kevin whether that was the point of it all. Because it seems a little, well, pointless.

"I don't care about likes or followers, at all. I care about consistency and brand voice and what we would call a brand story and strategy.

"Social media is this term that gets tossed around and some people have this mental block. I just view it as one of many communication tools some human beings use to connect, communicate - period. Radio is another. TVs another. Phone is another. Social media is just one of them.

"We just look at it in terms of trying to build relationships with people. That's it. Just be consistent and show up and do that in a relatable way.

What exactly constitutes relatable content? If some people had their way, the Internet would be full of only cat photos. Some days it already is.

"The differentiating factor in your business, for nine out of ten small to mid-size businesses, is staring back at you in the mirror. We don't communicate and connect with each other as human beings the way we advertise at each other. The real trick is to get people to be themselves, which doesn't necessarily mean always just posting their own photo over their own thoughts. But who they are, what their values are, what they stand for, what it was that got them into business, what keeps them going.

"There's something deeper there that's a reflection, I believe, of those people and their personality and what they value and, frankly, what they don't. That's what I'm trying to find and then communicate that in a human way, the way that a human will talk, not the way social media or marketing sounds or looks. Because most of that is just nonsense.

"In terms of what you put out there, your brand story is you. That's who you are. That's what you're really selling."

"Do we (at NSM Brand Media) sell social media marketing services? That's one of them but what we're really selling is support and encouragement and coaching and what kinds of problems you're solving and pain points that you take away."

Kevin acknowledges that the most difficult thing for his clients to wrap their heads around is how to present themselves authentically. It's curious that being oneself is the toughest part of it all.

"Pre-pandemic when I was doing a lot of talks about marketing - and that's starting to come back now – the top question that I would always get asked is not how does the algorithm work or, how much should I spend on Google Ad words, or Facebook pay-per-click? Or what trend should I chase or what channel should I use? Or any of that. The top question by far was always, what do I say?

"There's an interesting irony in that question. What happens is that when it comes time to put the message out, we look around at what others are doing. We do this in our own lives as well because we think they must have it figured out. And then come up with some version of what looks like marketing or sounds like social media. But most of it is nonsense.

"When I was selling radio, I'd get orders for radio advertising campaigns for tens of thousands of dollars. They'd buy the airtime; they'd pay the bill, and I'd have to chase them for what we used to call ad copy. They didn't know what they wanted to say. Well, that's ass backwards.

"So many of us grew up in this this top-of-mind awareness game of the 20th century, but it's not the

1990s anymore. I'm aware of all kinds of businesses that I don't care about and would rather they go out of my awareness. What I'm interested in is connection."

Kevin says it's about authenticity and relatability. What a business owner, potential influencer, or anyone hoping to gain traction from their social media needs to do is create and nurture relationships.

"I skewer industry jargon in my talks, and it gets lots of laughs because everybody recognizes when you put it in front of them. For example, a radio ad that's burned into my memory. 'Innovative engineering. Award-winning design. And right now, you can experience the sheer passion of driving an all-new IS-300 with lease rates as low as $200 bi-weekly.'"

In his live presentation, Kevin presents the ridiculousness of that verbiage on a human level.

"When has there ever been a time when two people are sitting at the kitchen table and they're talking about getting a new vehicle. "It needs to have more innovative engineering!" It always gets a laugh because people don't talk like that.

"But that's how marketing sounds. Car dealerships are the most obvious examples. In this case, the car company has this product that they want me to care about. If I can take the name of it and swap it out for a Star Wars robot without losing any context of the message, there's a jargon problem. Get new lease rates on a new R2D2! I don't know what an IS-300 is. Is it an SUV, is it a car, is it two doors, is it four, is it sport? I don't know. I know that you know. But I'm the one that needs to know because you're trying to sell me your stuff. It's got no context. That's not how people talk."

Kevin shares how he would coach that client into trading industry terminology for a more relatable message about the new car.

"Does it look cool? Does it go fast? Is it easy to hook up the Bluetooth on my phone? Does it have heated seats? A backup camera? That's how people talk. We don't say, only for a limited time. Hurry. Rush - right now. Yes, because that's what you appreciate most from people, right? Is when they nag, shame, and rush you.

"We must work people through the discomfort of not doing that (using jargon) because they're so used to it without even recognizing that they've completely tuned out that messaging in their own lives. Until it's time to put a message out themselves and then they don't trust themselves. Because they don't know what to say."

NSM tracks data for every client, every month. They have a clear understanding of what works and what doesn't when it comes to social media. Kevin says one type of posting performs well ahead of all others, no matter who posts it. Be it a real estate brokerage, a B2B consultancy, or even a car dealership.

"Candid photos of people smiling. And if there's more than one person in it, it will do better than just one person."

If you break out into a flop sweat at the thought of putting a photo or video of you out for public consumption, you're not alone. Everyone thinks they're the only ones who look 'bad' in pictures and videos, but Kevin says it's a universal reaction.

"Every single person we've worked with, including myself for our own channels, judges themselves relentlessly. They hate seeing their own photo or seeing themselves on video. Men, women, blue collar, white collar – it doesn't matter. None of them think that they're good enough.

"First of all, I would never use anything that I thought wasn't in the best interest of the client. Why would I try to make a client look bad? So, let's unpack this for a second. I'm an example of a person who's seeing this and what I see is you. The person that I love, admire, and respect. I'm choosing to use this piece of content because it's relatable. It's human. You're the one judging yourself based on what you think other people might think.

"The irony is, you're trying to get their attention. You're worried about what they're going to think but they're thinking about themselves. Consider what's on your mind as you go about the day. You're just trying to survive and get through the stuff that you've got to do. And, for anyone who would judge you, why would you want to attract them to your business anyway? Let them go."

Kevin and his team view social media as a simple tool. They break it down for people who are nervous about what their content should include. Knowing there's an ocean of people in the same business or category, all vying for attention, Kevin cuts to the core of what breaks through.

"If you're in real estate for instance, most people are not in the market to buy or sell a home right now. They will be a 'tomorrow customer.' But everybody's shouting the same thing that most people aren't really interested in right now. In the case of real estate, it's market stats, just sold, just listed, open houses – it's part of the machinery of that industry so I'm not saying don't do it. But show some personality, show who you are, show some relatability so that people might be entertained or engaged or feel some sense of connection with you.

"We've got real estate clients. Two videos for our one brokerage client have racked up tens of thousands of views. We do all the market updates and everything that you can think of regarding real estate. But their most popular videos were asking what's your favorite flavor of ice cream, and it's Friday night, what drink are you ordering?

"Why? Because it's relatable. Or when you ask somebody, what's a movie that you've seen ten times or more, but when it comes on late at night you'll still watch it. Why do you keep going back to it? Stuff like that always does well because it's relatable. It's fun. It's interesting. It tells you a bit about the person's personality and who they are and who they're not. Don't post that kind of stuff seven days a week. But mix it in. We're afraid to, thinking, I've got to have a call to action. I've got to ask for a sale with every single post. That's a sure-fire way to drive people away."

The "always be closing" attitude on social media isn't only a huge turnoff, it simply doesn't work, says Kevin. It kills any chance of a human-to-human moment.

"If you've ever been in sales you know that a small percentage of the communication is asking for the order. Most of it's just getting to know each other. Relationship building. And that's how we do social media. Build relationships. Be reciprocal. And be strategic about building in the call to actions but do that in a relatable and a human way. And so far so good.

"I'm not trying to create an influencer. I could give a tinker's flip about the latest trend or dance but if that's fun for you, it's part of your personality and you want to build that in, do it! But don't do it because you think that you must, or you're supposed to. Or get yourself tied in knots about trying to hack the algorithm or go viral.

"Think of it like planting seeds rather than buying lottery tickets. Just keep showing up. Consistency and staying on voice surpass all of it. Gimmicks are in there with advertising cliches and industry jargon. Trying to market with gimmicks is like trying to remember what lie you told last. You run out of rope."

If doing this was easy – finding your own authentic voice and just being yourself – NSM Brand Media would be out of business. But Kevin acknowledges that it's hard for most people to strip away everything they think they should be doing and find their true selves under all that clutter.

"It is a challenge to write and communicate in your own voice. You read someone's website or the way they write a social media post and think, is that really you? Is that what you would say if I were sitting across the table having coffee with you or is it what you think you should say? Just be yourself and the rest will come."

Chapter Six

The Interview

You've made it to the studio, and you're about to be interviewed. Now what? How can you make it the best it can be?

BASIC DETAILS

First thing to do: show up! If you're coming in for a morning show, reception won't be open yet. Have you been told how you'll get in the building? Which door to use? Is there an intercom? Where can you park? What number do you call if you need to talk to someone because of an emergency or delay? (Please don't have an emergency or a delay!) Who are you meeting? Who will interview you? What is the show called? Will there be a call-in portion of the segment or is it a straight interview? Make sure you know all these things before your appearance.

If you're asked to show up at eight, please arrive at eight. Not 7:50 and not 8:05. The host or producer may be dealing with a guest ahead of you and not have time to talk to you yet. If you show up late, you might miss your segment altogether while they're busy filling in the time on air. Another upside of podcasting is that it's prerecorded, and it can live forever. We used to joke that on the radio, we made air. Once it went out on the airwaves, it was gone forever.

In my last show's case, we were a skeleton crew. If someone turned up when we were all on the air, there was no one available to let them in. Many times, a guest arrived early and stood outside in the subzero winter cold, getting upset because they couldn't get in until the exact time they were told. Live broadcasting exists minute to minute. If we say you'll be on air at 8:07, we mean 8:07, not 8:03 or 8:10.

If you're being interviewed by phone, an old-fashioned landline is preferable to a cellphone. If you must use a cell, please don't move around, or multitask. First, if you are on the move it will be obvious. Extend the courtesy of being in the moment and concentrating on the interview. Second, moving just a few feet away might affect the cell signal. A dropped signal is annoying for everyone, especially the listener.

> *"If you are lucky enough to be asked to call in or appear in studio, remember the call letters while on air." — Rob Murphy, Host, D-Moos Radio*

How will you remember your interview time? An alarm in your phone or on your calendar is a great idea. Do you have a backup number? Create a plan b in case your battery dies, and we can't reach you. Better yet, get it fully charged ahead of time. Are they calling you or are you calling in? Disable call waiting or any other feature that will make noise or cause you to drop out. Quality is the key when it comes to being on the air or recorded.

The top irritants in interviews of any kind are harsh and unexplained noises. Please don't clear your throat on the air. Some people do it regularly, and don't even notice, as part of their personal speech pattern. PR reps need to make them aware of it so they can quit the bad habit. (It's also hard on the vocal cords.) Ninety percent of the time, a problem with a guest's throat is a combination of nerves and dryness. If you're offered water, take it. Keeping the throat lubricated ought to eliminate hoarseness. If you get the feeling that something is closing in on your throat, take a sip of water. Swallow hard. Try not to make a throat-clearing sound on the air because I promise you, it's a huge turnoff. If you must do it, turn your head from the mic or phone while you do.

Find out how long the interview will last. This will help you gauge the level of detail you'll be able to get into during your chat. Remember my earlier suggestion about drafting an e-mail pitch and pretending you must hold someone's attention in a conversation? Well, this is the real thing. It is a conversation. You'll be on a microphone, not a megaphone, and you aren't expected to be anything except yourself. The more relaxed, genuine, informed, prepared and down-to-earth you are, the better you will come across.

INTERVIEW FAIL

Before we get to more details about a good interview, let me tell you about a terrible one.

The writer of a play that was being launched in Toronto came in to talk about it. He had hopes of taking *Tiananmen Dreams* to Broadway, and his ambition was palpable. He also had a massive ego and expected to become the next Andrew Lloyd Webber. I introduced him as the creator and writer of *Tiananmen Dreams* and asked for his inspiration. He began:

"Well, *Tiananmen Dreams*, which I wrote the book and lyrics to …"

I could almost hear the eyes of our station's listeners glazing over. Mine certainly were. What's more, he proceeded to mention the play's name in every sentence. It wasn't a conversation; it was an ad and a poorly written one. The play was about the Tiananmen Square Massacre of 1989, a remarkable point in history and an incredible, tragic story. But this guy reduced it to a me-me-me moment and blew his opportunity. He didn't make a connection with me or the audience. I kept trying to drag him into a human-style conversation, and he kept sounding like a snake-oil salesperson. If you're wondering why you've never heard of *Tiananmen Dreams*, it's because the play was an insufferable disaster that was savaged by critics and closed early. I barely made it through the first half of a preview before bolting from the theatre.

Some authors, musicians, and others over the years have also given this type of interview. They've been nervous and wanted to make sure that the name of their project was mentioned enough times. But they didn't touch an emotion or create a relatable moment. They tried to sell-sell-sell, and that simply doesn't work. Listeners and viewers can hear and see right through an attempt to shove a hand in their wallet. They need to get something out of the experience of listening or they'll vanish. The first question they want answered is, "What's in this for me?" It always goes back to telling a good story.

. . .

TRUST YOUR BROADCASTING PROFESSIONAL OR HOST

The least-experienced guests are the most difficult to deal with. They're overly concerned about what they're going to say, and worse, what we're going to say, projecting their inexperience onto us. Asking if we're prepared to give the website and show times is one thing. Telling us how and when to say them is another that's overbearing and not appreciated. Sometimes, one must trust that others know how to do their job. I conducted interviews for several hours every day and more years than I care to count. I'm certainly capable of making a mistake, but I don't need to be ridden like a horse in the Kentucky Derby over details to remember them.

If a host happens to make a mistake, a gentle correction is much better than a full stop to say, "You made a mistake!" Be kind. If you're on a podcast, know that edits can be made before the episode is released. Mistakes are rarely fatal.

Once you have developed a rapport with a producer or a host, it's tempting to go off the record with delicious details or secrets that you don't want to put out for public knowledge. The only way to ensure that your confidence is kept is to not give into temptation. However, we all love to dish a little dirt, and if you do decide to share something privately, make it clear that it's confidential. Say the actual words: "This is off the record." Never assume. I've seen someone's deep secret get the full on-air treatment because they assumed the person they were telling would know it wasn't for public consumption.

If you think you might get asked something you don't want to answer, prepare a response such as, "I haven't made up my mind on that yet." or "I'm not prepared to discuss that right now." Whatever is appropriate to the situation. Be polite, but firm. You are in charge of what you say. It's better to not say anything than to say something you'll regret or make something up when you don't know the answer. "I don't know." is perfectly acceptable when it's honest.

A GREAT GUEST:

- Knows their stuff.

- Has anecdotes ready to go.

- Makes their material relatable to the average person.

- Has passion for the topic. And if not passion, displays a genuine interest in it.

. . .

WHAT DOESN'T BELONG

Inside jokes. Anything that was said before the show or in another interview. Never (and I mean ever!) say, "We were talking off air …" We keep the perception that nothing worthwhile happens off the air. To the listener or viewer, the show is all there is. Don't leave them out, wondering what goes on when the mics go off and the lights go dim. If you want to reference something that was previously discussed, don't say, "as we were talking about before the show." Just simply bring it into the conversation.

If necessary, a good host will help make you look and sound good and fill in gaps if your memory fails. Unless you're on the hot seat for a controversial issue, that is. And in that case, you wouldn't have been brought in by a publicist, and you'll expect some heat. Elected officials are on their own.

But, if a guest falters, they're safe. We want the segment to go well

PRACTICE MAKES PERFECT

On the other hand, if you're being pushed out in front, and you're not ready for prime time, it's better to gain some experience by practicing first. Many PR reps will conduct a mock interview and deliver feedback.

A first-time author once appeared on my radio talk show, and she was so nervous that she was only capable of making noises, not full sentences. I went to a commercial break and tried to talk her down off the ledge. She assured me she was okay. We came back from the break, and her nonsensical freak-out continued. It truly was gibberish. I ended up briefly describing the book and cutting the segment short. The author was in tears. She never should have been put in that position. Someone took her money and promised her press coverage but didn't ascertain her capabilities and readiness for publicity. I didn't blame the author; I blamed the publicist.

The questions in the interview might not be chronological. Perhaps the interviewer won't start at the beginning. They might begin with something they find more compelling, with a goal of grabbing the attention of the listener, viewer or reader and convincing them to stay for the rest. This is what we do. Try to have some fun. Everyone worries about making a mistake, but mistakes are human and can be corrected. It's better to sound like you're in a natural conversation than to be robotic and perfect. Live in the moment. Listen. React. It's a conversation, not a lecture. To quote a great saying, "Don't let perfect be the enemy of good."

. . .

COMPETITION AGAIN

Once you get on the air, never, ever refer to another media company or competing podcast. If you have done so in my presence, know that while a smile was plastered on my face, I was fantasizing about unleashing my wrath. Competitors include print and television that are not "in the family" and owned by the same company. They also include satellite radio.

Think of it this way: you wouldn't hear someone reading the flyer specials from one grocery store on the in-store sound system at its major competitor. Media competitors are the same, and that includes Canada's CBC. (Private radio's relationship with the government-funded CBC is complicated. Private radio pros respect and often admire the talented people who create the programming, but bristle at the business model. Briefly, CBC does not have to play commercials to survive, usually has more staff, competes for ratings, then brags if they win by buying ads and billboards with tax dollars. Many in private broadcasting don't think that's fair.)

You won't hear one company promote the events of another and vice versa. Promotional sponsorships by broadcast outlets are partly in place to protect an event from the other company's involvement. So, you will understand why you shouldn't mention an earlier interview with a host from another station when you're on with us.

In one city where I worked, the official New Year's Eve celebration was always hosted by an announcer from a competitor. Everyone on the organizing committee knew that when they talked on air with us about the night's programming, the name of that host was simply never brought up. The other station would demand the same courtesy if one of our hosts had been involved. We don't acknowledge each other publicly. It's just how it's done.

Chapter Seven

Barb Botten—Marketing Advice for the Business Guest

"Emotional marketing is something that some businesses don't value as much as branding, but emotional connections transcend brands. They deliver beyond our expectations of great performance. They reach our heart, as well as our mind, creating an intimate, responsive connection that you just can't live without.

Take a brand away, and people will find a replacement. Take that emotional connection away, and people will protest its absence. You don't just listen to an emotional connection; you embrace it passionately. Your marketing offers the unique ability to tell your story in such a way that it creates that emotional connection if you let it.

It's been proven that brands that can master emotion have the potential to drive more sales.

When a brand makes us feel something, we carry it with us. We tell our family and friends; we share it on social networks. It makes us feel like we are part of something great, something that we can be passionate about.

Give your potential consumers what they want — a connection that is both meaningful and memorable.

Whatever your audience — radio listener, print reader or television viewer — focus on connecting with the audience's emotions." — Barb Botten, Editor/Publisher, Villager Publications

Conclusion

Bullet Points

Our first concern is what's in it for our listeners/viewers/readers. Answer that question in your pitch.

Remember the "elevator pitch." Don't bore us with details we don't need to know. Be concise.

An exceptional story well told is always compelling.

Give us lead time. We don't want to be late to the party, and it takes us a while to get ready.

Driving us nuts with e-mails or calls will not be to your benefit.

We talk to each other. We will share stories about you and your company if you deliberately set out to mislead us. (We will also share stories if you are impressive!)

Competition in the media is fierce. Respect it, please.

Do a little research to find out who we are, what our format is, the name of the show and our call letters or slogan.

Content is king. Lists of sponsors and sounding like a salesperson or a commercial will not help you or us. Be genuine. Be someone we want to spend time within a small room.

In the studio, have water at the ready, notes, a notepad and pen if you need it. Make eye contact. Be in the moment. Relax. It's a conversation. Connect. Be real. Be yourself.

Use social media. Look up our Instagram handles and Facebook pages. Like us, and we'll like you! Don't be afraid to be real. Connections are what matter on social media.

Everybody hates pictures and videos of themselves. Show up, be consistent and relatable.

Comments or questions? Find me on Facebook and Instagram. Follow me on Twitter. Visit me at voiceoflisabrandt.com.

Acknowledgements

Thanks first to my husband, Derek. He gives me encouragement and suggestions. He made this project — like he makes everything — better.

Thanks to my soul sister, Erin Davis, and her wonderful husband, Rob. They believe I can do anything I set my mind to. We should all have friends who are this delusional about our abilities. Erin retired from radio in 2016. She was the top morning show host in Toronto on CHFI for three decades. In 2019, she released the Canadian best-seller, *Mourning Has Broken: Love, Loss. and Reclaiming Joy*. Erin hosts several podcasts including her own, *Drift with Erin Davis* and *Gracefully and Frankly* with some woman named Lisa Brandt. Thank you, Erin for sharing your advice.

Thank you to Jason White and Barb Botten, for reading early drafts, offering suggestions, and contributing their expertise. Barb is the founder of Villager Publications. Thanks as well to contributors Dan Brown, Robyn Brady, and Rob Murphy. I have tremendous respect for all of you.

Thanks to Mark A. Rayner, for writing the foreword. I've read all of Mark's funny, intelligent novels and suggest that you do, too. Visit his website: markarayner. com. If you don't know where to start, I suggest *The Frigularity* or *The Fatness*.

Kevin Bulmer at NSM Brand Media is a great guy with a hundred talents who graciously shared his social media insight. Thanks, Kevin.

This guide started as a blog post at voiceoflisabrandt. com that attracted a bunch of shares and comments on social media. I finally got to work on it after some energizing and illuminating sessions with certified life coach Melissa Martin (www.martinwellness.ca) and some inspiration from the generous spirit of Tiffany Pringle-Austin.

My brother, Kevin, is always in my corner and cheering me on. He is an excellent writer and gives me great advice. My Mom was still with us during the first printing of this book. She was a tremendous source of support and I miss her terribly.

In April 2017, my dad, Jack, died after a long struggle with Parkinson's disease. He was always delighted by my writing and after reading one of my newspaper columns remarked, "I don't know how you're able to make a whole column out of something so small!" That was a compliment, Dad-style. His departure from this Earth has left an unfillable hole in my heart. This one's for you, Dad. Ten percent of net sales from this book go to the Parkinson's Rehab at Hotel Dieu Shaver Hospital in St. Catharines, Ontario, Canada. Dad attended the program and loved it. I deeply appreciate your support.

About the Author

LISA BRANDT was in radio for a long time although it's not true, as some have suggested, that she caught the sound of the big bang on her Radio Shack tape recorder.

She started out playing forty-fives and carts (Google them, kids!), progressed through CDs and survived well into the digital era. Her first radio interview was with The Irish Rovers on a cold, wintry day in Prince George, British Columbia. She picked them up at their hotel when neither the radio station nor the band would spring for a taxi. Band member Jimmy Ferguson got stuck in the front seat of her Chevy Monza when he moved it forward to let the other band members out of the tiny back seats. Lisa had to lean down between

Ferguson's legs and release the seat while he complained non-stop. Like most humiliating experiences, it became funny over time, and now it's one of her favorite stories.

Later, she appeared on various television projects, notably more than sixty episodes of Whatever Happened To? and she has written several regular newspaper columns on subjects as diverse as running a small business and home decor. Two of those columns were distributed nationally.

Throughout her radio career as a music-show host (DJ), talk-show host, newscaster, and producer, she has endured no-shows, miscommunications, begging, bribes, drunken guests, angry guests, unprepared guests, and those who had no idea why they were there. She has also conducted countless successful and pleasurable interviews with Canadian prime ministers, politicians, actors, singers, authors, and other fascinating people with exceptional stories to tell.

She also made her share of mistakes. But those are for another book.

Lisa lives in Port Stanley, Ontario, with her husband and their supervisory cat, Cuddles. She cohosts the podcast Gracefully and Frankly with Erin Davis. She's a voice-over artist, blogger, and content creator.

Check out her other books. *Celebrity Tantrums - The Official Dirt, The Naked Truth, Venus Rising, My Sepsis Story: How I Almost Died, and You Don't Have To* and *Trade Up: Why Buy a Job When You Can Start A Career.*

Connect with LISA BRANDT Online:

VoiceofLisaBrandt.com

Twitter.com/LisamBrandt

Facebook.com/Lisa.Brandt1

Instagram.com/LisamBrandt1